SWEET DREAMS, BOGIE…
I WILL BE READY

DULCES SUEÑOS, BOGIE…
ESTARÉ LISTO

Saying Goodbye To A Pet
Decir Adiós A Una Mascota

Written by | Escrito por: Marlana Leonard Illustrated by |Ilustrado por:Eloisa White

Sweet Dreams, Bogie...I Will Be Ready

Published by Gatekeeper Press
2167 Stringtown Rd, Suite 109
Columbus, OH 43123-2989
www.GatekeeperPress.com

ISBN (Hardcover): 9781642376746
ISBN (Paperback):9781642371925

Printed in the United States of America

Marlana Leonard

Was born and raised in California and remembers being surrounded by canine companions throughout her childhood. Bogie was Marlana's fondest canine friend who shared many life milestones with her. She received a B.A. in psychology and has taught elementary students for thirty years in California and New Mexico. Marlana is currently working as a holistic practitioner for animals and has taken over her late mother's website business (www.everglonaturalvet.com). She resides in California with her husband, Roger and their two dogs, Doc and Tinkerbell.

Marlana Leonard

Ella nació y creció en California y recuerda haber estado rodeado de compañeros caninos durante toda su infancia. Bogie era la amiga canina más querida de Marlana que compartió muchos hitos de la vida con ella. Ella recibió una B.A. en psicología y ha enseñado a estudiantes de primaria durante treinta años en California y Nuevo México. Marlana actualmente trabaja como practicante holística para animales y se ha hecho cargo del negocio de sitios web de su difunta madre (www.everglonaturalvet.com). Ella reside en California con su esposo, Roger y sus dos perros, Doc y Tinkerbell.

Eloisa White

Was born and raised in California. She has been drawing and painting since early childhood as a hobby, drawing for friends and for family. She majored in fashion design in California and finished her schooling in New Mexico. She and Marlana met at work in New Mexico and became friends. This is her first time illustrating for a book.

Eloisa White

Ella nació y creció en California. Ella ha estado dibujando y pintando desde la primera infancia como un hobby, dibujo para amigos y para la familia. Se especializó en diseño de moda en California y terminó su educación en Nuevo México. Ella y Marlana se conocieron en el trabajo en Nuevo México y se hicieron amigas. Esta es la primera vez ella ilustra para un libro.

DEDICATION – DEDICADO

Dedicated to my loving companion Bogie, who shared a part of my life for thirteen and a half years; a true friend to the end.
To my late sister Melinda, whom I believe is with Bogie waiting out there somewhere for me. Also, to my beloved husband Roger, for all his love and support. To Eloisa for her much-valued time in translating this book and her artistic talent in bringing Bogie to life on paper, to Frank Leene for his loving care of my little buddy, and my parents for all their love and support in writing this book. Thank you all, I appreciate your love and kindness!
Lastly, to my veterinarian Dr. Mike Dobesh, who is a caring and sensitive professional.
-You're awesome!
Love, M.L.

Dedicado a mi amoroso compañero Bogie, quien compartió una parte de mi vida durante trece años y medio; un verdadero amigo hasta el final
A mi difunta hermana Melinda, a quien creo que está con Bogie esperándome en alguna parte por mí.
También, a mi amado esposo Roger, por todo su amor y apoyo. A Eloisa por su tiempo tan valioso en la traducción de este libro y su talento artístico para darle vida a Bogie en papel, a Frank Leene por su amoroso cuidado de mi pequeño amigo y a mis padres por todo su amor y apoyo al escribir este libro. ¡Gracias a todos, aprecio su amor y amabilidad!
Por último, a mi veterinario, el Dr. Mike Dobesh, que es un profesional atento y sensible.
-¡Eres increíble!
Amor, M.L.

DEDICATION – DEDICADO

To my sweet Talis for your kind heart and love of animals which can be attributed to my childhood friend Lara. To my Robert who would watch me paint and always compliment my work, and who has the perfect timing when it comes to words I need to hear. To baby Madison, the three of us are eagerly awaiting your arrival, and I am proud to have a very special book we can read to you as you grow. Lastly, to my dear friend Marlana, thank you for the creative opportunity!
I love you all!
E.W.

A mi dulce Talis por su amable corazón y amor por los animales que pueden atribuirse a mi amiga de la infancia Lara. Para mi Robert, que me miraba pintar y siempre complementa mi trabajo, y que tiene el tiempo perfecto cuando se trata de palabras que necesito escuchar. Para el bebé Madison, los tres estamos esperando ansiosamente su llegada, y me enorgullece tener un libro muy especial que podamos leer mientras crece. Por último, a mi querida amiga Marlana, ¡gracias por la oportunidad creativa!
-¡Los amo a todos!
E.W.

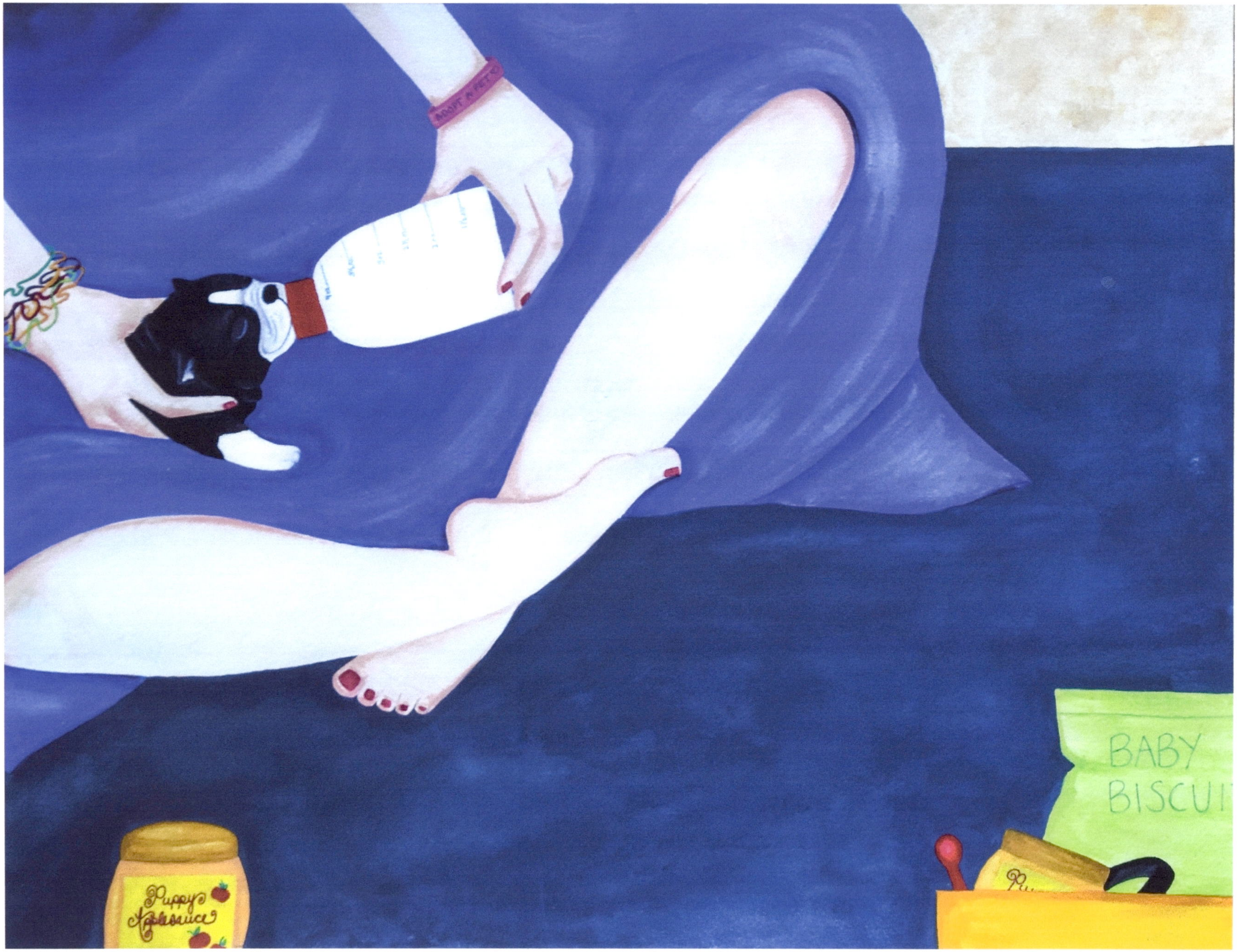

Puppy Applesauce
BABY BISCUI

When I saw you the first time and
held you in my hands, I knew we
were going to be great friends, and
I was so excited!

*Cuando te vi la primera vez y te
sostuve en mis manos, supe que
íbamos a ser grandes amigos, y
¡estaba tan emocionada!*

I took you home and watched you
nestle into your little bed with the look
of happiness on your face. I felt like a
new mom, and I was really proud.

*Te llevé a casa y te vi acurrucada en tu
pequeña cama con la expresión de
felicidad en tu rostro. Me sentí como una
nueva mamá, y estaba muy orgullosa.*

B
is for Bogie
It's a Boy!
BABY
Biscui

You slowly became used to
your leash and we went on
many walks together, and I
was looking forward to
many more.

Poco a poco te acostumbraste a tu correa e hicimos muchas caminatas juntos, y esperaba muchas más.

I took you to the vet to get
your shots and check-ups,
and you weren't really
happy during these visits.

*Te lleve al veterinario para tus
vacunas y examenes, y no
estabas tan alegre durante estas
citas.*

"DOG VISION EXAM"
HOW TO CARE FOR ♥ A PET ♥
1. LOVE AND ATTENTION.
2. DIET AND EXERCISE.
3. PROPER GROOMING CARE.
4. SHELTER.
5. PICK A GREAT VETERINARIAN!

Many times, you insisted on
going "bye-bye" with me in the
truck (and of course you
had to bring your beloved
chewy along), and we
enjoyed going on many
adventures together.

Muchas veces, insististe en irte
"adiósito" conmigo en el camión (y,
por supuesto, tenías que traer a tu
amado masticable), y disfrutamos
de muchas aventuras juntos.

As you grew older, we
helped each other go
through difficult times.

A medida que crecías, nos
ayudábamos mutuamente en
tiempos difíciles.

We also went through many
happy times,
and I valued our friendship.

También pasamos por muchos
momentos felices,
y valoré nuestra amistad.

We loved dressing up
together: Your favorite outfit
was a dark blue hoodie
sweatshirt, mine was
carrying you in my baby
shoulder carrier.

*Nos encanto vestirnos juntos:
Tu ropa favorita era tu sueter
azul marino con caperuza; la
mia era cargandote en un
sostenedorde bebes.*

We moved to different houses,

and it was comforting to know you were by my side.

Nos mudamos a diferentes casas,

y fue reconfortante saber que estabas a mi lado.

We even moved to another state.

Incluso nos mudamos a otro estado.

Wyoming
NOW LEAVING THE GOLDEN STATE
CALIFORNIA
Nevada
Utah
Colorado
MOVE-IT
YOUR SELF CO.
1-800-123-MOVE
Arizona
DESTINATION LAND OF ENCHANTMENT
Santa Fe
NEW MEXICO
PACIFIC OCEAN

In your golden years, you became friends with another doggie named Brownie and we were accepted as part of a larger family, and we were at peace and happy.

En tus años dorados, te hiciste amigo de otro perrito llamado Brownie y fuimos aceptados como parte de una familia más grande, y estábamos en paz y felices.

Many years later, as all living creatures must, you grew very tired and became ill. You could no longer eat, became weak, and stopped jumping like you used to when greeting me home, and I was trying to be ready.

Muchos años después, como deben hacerlo todas las criaturas vivientes, te cansaste y enfermaste. No podía comer, te debilitaste y dejaste de saltar como lo habías hecho cuando me saludaba en casa, y yo estaba tratando de estar lista.

Then, one cold, cloudy,
and windy Fall afternoon
in November, just before
Thanksgiving, I had to make
an unselfish choice. You were
ready, and I was gathering
strength to be ready.

*Luego, una fría, nublada, y
ventosa tarde de otoño en
noviembre, justo antes del Día
de Acción de Gracias, yo tuve
que hacer una decision dificil.
Estabas listo, y yo estuve
reuniendo fuerzas para estar lista.*

I took you to your favorite vet
so that you could be at
peace, my dear companion
…and we were both ready.

*Te llevé a tu veterinario favorito
para que pudieras estar en paz,
mi querido compañero
…y ambos estábamos listos.*

Now I look back on the days
we shared, and I am
thankful you came into my
life. I miss you very much
and you will always be in my
heart and memories.

*Ahora miro hacia atrás en los
días que comdartimos, y estoy
agradecido de que hayas
entrado en mi vida. Te extraño
mucho y siempre estarás en mi
corazón y mis recuerdos.*

I know someday I will see you again my little friend,
and when that time comes…

*Sé que algún día te veré de nuevo mi pequeño amigo,
y cuando llegue ese momento …*

Bogie
memorabilia
PHOTO
ALBUM

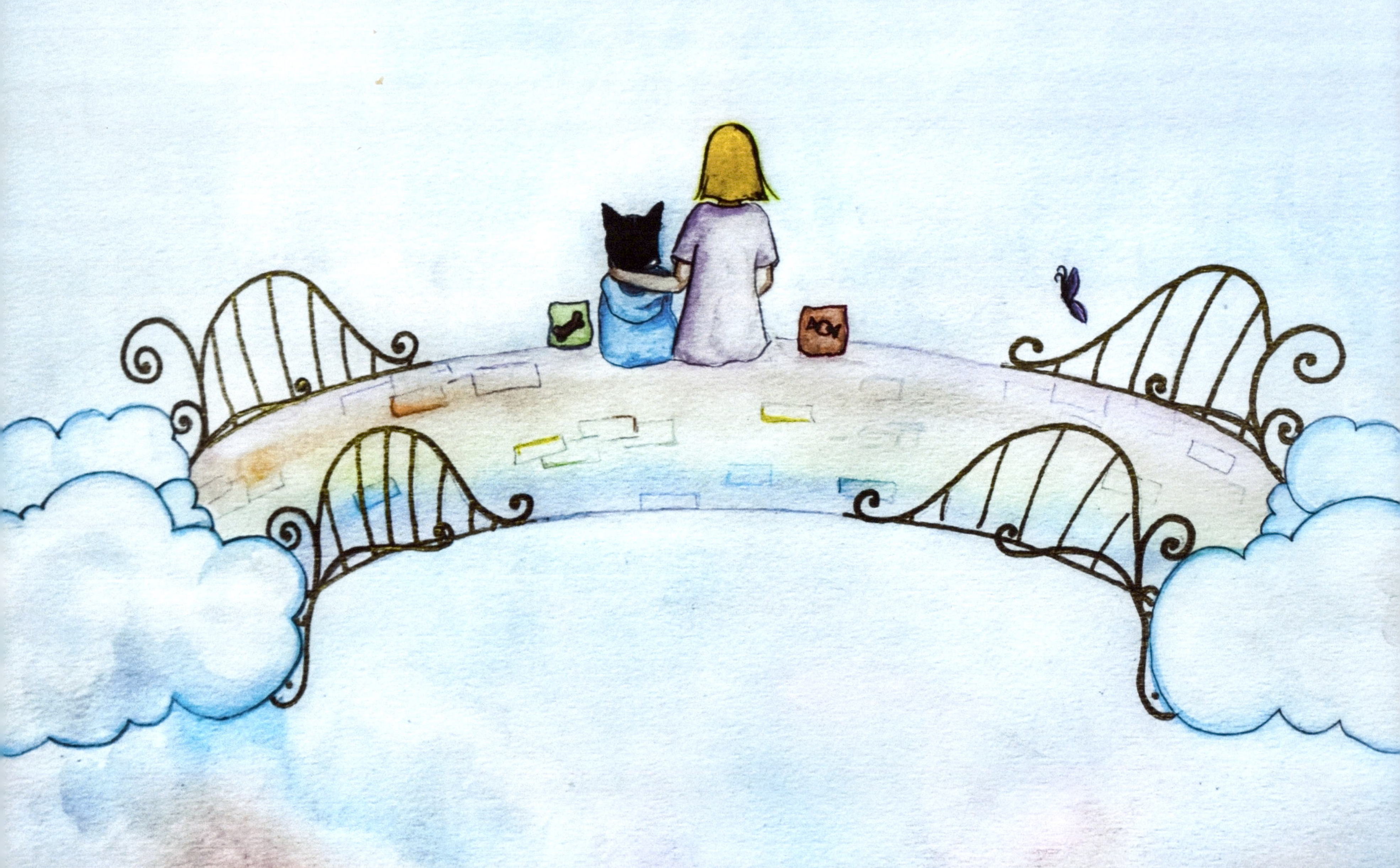

I will be ready!

¡Estaré listo!